GLITTER EVERYWHERE!

Where It Came From,
Where It's Found
& Where It's Going

See Title!

Chris Barton

Illustrated by **Chaaya Prabhat**

Charlesbridge

For Harold Underdown, from many angles—C. B.

For my best friend, Arthi, for pretending
to like my glittery nails—C. P.

Published by Charlesbridge
9 Galen Street
Watertown, MA 02472
(617) 926-0329
www.charlesbridge.com

Printed in China
(hc) 10 9 8 7 6 5 4 3 2 1

Illustrations done in digital media
Display type hand-lettered by Chaaya Prabhat and
    set in Jellygest Fat by Jakob Fischer
Text type set in Museo Slab by Jos Buivenga
Printed by 1010 Printing International Limited
    in Huizhou, Guangdong, China
Production supervision by Jennifer Most Delaney
Designed by Jon Simeon

Special thanks to astrophysicist Dr. Carlos Bacigalupo
for sharing his expertise on color, light, and reflection.

Library of Congress Cataloging-in-Publication Data
Names: Barton, Chris, author. | Prabhat, Chaaya, illustrator.
Title: Glitter everywhere!: where it came from, where it's found & where it's going /
    Chris Barton; illustrated by Chaaya Prabhat.
Description: Watertown, MA: Charlesbridge, [2023] | Includes bibliographical
    references. | Audience: Ages 5–9 years | Audience: Grades 2–3 | Summary:
    "An informative picture book about the origins and present-day uses of—
    and obsession with—glitter."—Provided by publisher.
Identifiers: LCCN 2021031155 (print) | LCCN 2021031156 (ebook) |
    ISBN 9781623542528 (hardcover) | ISBN 9781632897831 (ebook)
Subjects: LCSH: Glitter art—Juvenile literature. | Decoration and ornament—
    Juvenile literature.
Classification: LCC TT880 .B325 2023 (print) | LCC TT880 (ebook) | DDC 745.5—
    dc23/eng/20211006
LC record available at https://lccn.loc.gov/2021031155
LC ebook record available at https://lccn.loc.gov/2021031156

Many thanks to the many people who aided my research in ways large and small, including Lauren
Antolino at the Cranford Public Library; Jacqueline Artier at the Bibliothèque interuniversitaire
de la Sorbonne; Pat Bankowski, Tammy Shaw, and Ryan Scott Weber at the Bernardsville Public
Library; Gilly Barnes; Hillary Belzer of the Makeup Museum; Steven Bibb and Mary Direnzo at
the Fashion Institute of Technology; Nick Brown; Ty Burns; Kimberly Carrillo at the Cupcake
Bar; George Chrisman of the National Fishing Lure Collectors Club; Mary L. Chute, Leigh Clark,
Regina Fitzpatrick, and Sharon Rawlins at the New Jersey State Library; Joan Regan Enyingi; Dr.
Dannielle Green at Anglia Ruskin University; Rose Mary Hoge at the Cleveland Public Library;
Soline Holmes and Alicia Schwarzenbach of the Krewe of Muses; Dr. Salima Ikram and Dr. André
J. Veldmeijer of the Tutankhamun Sticks and Staves Project; Teri Kandel at the Cranford Historical
Society; Bill Kimack; Dr. Gene Kritsky at Mount St. Joseph University; L. Michele Lawrie-Munro at
the American Institute of Mining, Metallurgical, and Petroleum Engineers; Tara Lazar; Judith K.
Levine; Joan and Don Lyons at the Heddon Museum; Dr. Lise Manniche; Dr. Robert Mensah-Biney
at North Carolina State University; Maria Montesano at Cornell University; Martina Mrongovius
at the Center for the Holographic Arts; Marianna Naum at the US Food and Drug Administration;
Diana Craig Patch at the Metropolitan Museum of Art; Sandy Stuart Perry; Marc Pierce at the
University of Texas at Austin; Darla Rance at the Helen Hall Library; Mai Reitmeyer at the American
Museum of Natural History; Dr. David Rivers at Loyola University Maryland; Pam Robinson at the
Somerset County Historical Society; Roberta Ruschmann at Meadowbrook Inventions; Nicole
Seymour, author of Glitter in Bloomsbury's Object Lessons book series; Mark Smith, formerly at
the Texas State Library and Archives; Susan Enyingi Spencer; Christine Taylor-Butler; Samantha
Thomas at Colorlord Limited; Judy Weiner; and helpful folks whose names I did not catch at the
Bernards Township Library, the Newark Public Library, and the Perry-Castañeda Library at the
University of Texas at Austin.—C. B.

Glitter is lots of things.
Tiny.
Clingy.
Colorful.
Loved.

Not loved.

And believe me, we're going to talk about *all* of that. But glitter is something else, too.

Iridescent.

Iridescence is why so many of us are attracted to glitter.

Iridescence is when light and color seem to shape-shift across a surface.

"Attracted to glitter" might be putting it mildly. For some among us, "obsessed with glitter" is more like it. You know who you are.

It captures the eye. It mesmerizes.

Iridescence is . . .

what makes glitter sparkle.

When light waves hit an object, some of them are absorbed and some are reflected. We see the reflected light.

SPECTRUM OF VISIBLE LIGHT

BLUE LIGHT REFLECTED

An iridescent surface reflects light in a special way called interference. The light waves combine, sometimes growing stronger together and sometimes canceling each other out.

The object looks brighter or dimmer from even slightly different angles. Turn it just a little, and it brightens then dims then brightens again. It glitters.

This isn't magic, or fairy dust, or unicorn dandruff. It's science.

We humans are drawn to sparkly things.

Our brains may associate that shimmer with light reflecting off the surface of water. Water is essential to life, so it makes sense that we would take a shine to it.

Or maybe we just like sparkly things because they're beautiful, or because they give us another tool for expressing ourselves.

Whatever the reason, people's love of glitter goes way back.

At least as far back as . . . beetles.

Beetles?

Yes, beetles.

There are hundreds of thousands of types of beetles, and many types are iridescent.

SPECTRUM OF VISIBLE LIGHT

REFLECTED LIGHT

ABSORBED LIGHT

A beetle's outer wings, called elytra, are made up of many thin layers. Each layer reflects the light a little differently. Seen from different angles, the beetle can seem to shine like a jewel. This multilayer reflection is basically how modern glitter works.

More than three thousand years ago, Egyptians placed sticks decorated with colorful little pieces of cut-up beetle wings in the tomb of the pharaoh Tutankhamun. Even now, archaeologists studying those sticks can see that glittery, beetle-y effect.

Like today's glitter fans, ancient Egyptians clearly saw value in the tiny and shiny.

Also in the Tiny & Shiny section of human history, we find the mineral mica. Because of the way its thin layers reflect light, specks of mica have long been used all over the world to add a glittery effect to artwork and other creations.

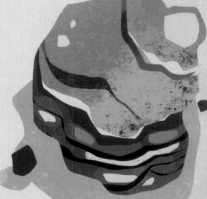

Mica has been found in cave paintings in South Africa, in ancient Greek pottery, in dyes from China's Han dynasty, and on the walls of old Mayan temples.

In the late 1700s a Japanese artist known as Sharaku used mica to create the sparkly black backgrounds in his famous portraits of kabuki actors.

For centuries mica has lent a silvery or golden sheen to many fabrics in India.

In the United States in the early 1900s, mica was used in greeting cards, artificial snow, and holiday ornaments. Manufacturers cut mica, metal, and paper into tiny pieces they called . . . flitter.

No, not glitter. Not yet.

The verb "glitter" comes from the Middle English word "gliteren," meaning to flash or sparkle. The noun "flitter" is a German word for tinsel, which comes from the verb "flittern," which likewise means to sparkle. So what does that mean for "glitter" and "flitter"? Hardly anything! It's just a quirk of history that these two rhyming words from different languages came to refer to the same stuff—and that "glitter" eventually won out.

Christmas **SNOW**

At that time "flitter" was the more common name for flecks of shiny mica and whatnot. Sure, flitter was glitterish. You could even say that flitter glittered. But for now that shimmer mainly came from flitter, not glitter.

WAR MATERIALS

MICA

During World War II the US military needed lots of mica for use in electronics and other equipment.

The time was right for someone to come up with an alternative to mica for use as glitter—er, *flitter*. War or no war, folks still wanted to be festive.

What about glass as an alternative to mica? Glitter made of silver-coated crushed glass does have a certain shimmer to it. But Germany was the main producer of glass glitter, and in the 1940s that country was at war with the United States and its allies. Also, no matter how carefully you handle glass glitter, it's still CRUSHED GLASS.

Enter Henry F. Ruschmann, a German immigrant who invented a machine for cutting up leftover scraps of thin plastic into tiny bits that sparkled in the light.

Henry F. Ruschmann didn't call those bits flitter . . .

He called them slivers.

In 1943 Henry F. Ruschmann and his wife, Bertha, bought a 252-acre cattle farm in the small town of Bernardsville, New Jersey.

In one room of their new home on Meadowbrook Farm, he put his new invention to work producing slivers—not just for cards and ornaments, but also for jewelry and fishing lures.

Sometimes in nonfiction books, I refer to people by just their first names to help create a sense of connection with them. You'll meet "Leonard" and "Judy" in this book, but not simply "Henry." Henry F. Ruschmann never said much about himself, and his family doesn't say much about him, either. There's just not a lot that we know about the man.

That's why this book refers to Henry F. Ruschmann as "Henry F. Ruschmann." I like to think that Henry F. Ruschmann would have wanted it that way.

Yes, whatever he called it, he was making glitter inside the house. How do you think *that* went over?

Henry F. Ruschmann moved his glitter machine into a nearby building.

Eight decades later, glitter is still made on Meadowbrook Farm.

Riding down the highway today, you'd never know that you're passing by a glitter factory. And not just any glitter factory—the birthplace of modern glitter. The rolling green land still looks like just a cattle farm.

Henry F. Ruschmann's lack of flash was on full display when he died in 1989. Three local newspapers ran obituaries about him—and not one of them included the word "glitter" (or even "slivers"). His gravestone, too, gives no hint that it marks the resting place of the father of modern glitter.

What's more, Henry F. Ruschmann called his business Meadowbrook Inventions. This goes to show that a flashy product like glitter doesn't necessarily come from a company with a flashy name.

But the business attracted attention all the same.

As Meadowbrook's glitter (and, gradually, the term "glitter") became more popular, along came competition.

In New York in the late 1950s, Leonard Getler and Morris Kirshen created a company they named Magic Sparkles (awesome) to make what they called . . . flitter (whoops).

In 1963 Leonard Getler formed a new company called . . . Glitterex. (Too bad, Flitterex.) Like Meadowbrook Inventions, Glitterex began in New Jersey. But that's not all they have in common. These rivals—and the people who run them today—tend to say very little about their businesses. They prefer to let their glitter speak—or sparkle—for itself.

"My father always came home with glitter on him," recalls Leonard's daughter Judy.

As a girl, Judy would visit Magic Sparkles, put her hands into a huge drum of glitter, and fling its contents into the air.

That's one way to make a floor shine!

In the early days, making glitter was fairly simple. Machines cut big pieces of film into smaller, circular pieces. But that meant the material between the circles went unused.

To avoid waste, glitter factories switched to shapes with straight sides. Rolls of aluminum or plastic were fed through a machine that sliced the thin sheets this way and that into rectangles and squares (and later, hexagons).

Over time and around the world, some glitter makers started using sheets made up of several super-thin layers of plastic that each reflect light differently, kind of like the iridescent wings of a beetle.

They also began making glitter from plastic sheets coated with vaporized metal. A lightweight layer of aluminum makes the glitter extra glossy.

Now factories even use film embossed with holographic patterns that split white light into a rainbow of color.

We keep discovering ways of making glitter ever more glittery!

Improvements in technology have also allowed glitter to get more minuscule.

Glitter used in craft products is usually as small as 375 microns across and 150 microns thick. That's pretty tiny. You'd have to stack around 169 pieces one on top of the other (good luck with that!) to wind up with a glitter tower one inch high.

You probably aren't used to thinking of sizes in terms of microns—unless you're in the habit of thinking about really, really small things. How small? The thickness of this page you're reading is around 152 microns. That's more than twelve times thicker than the thinnest glitter, such as a kind used in aerosol sprays.

But craft glitter is a lot bigger than other types of glitter, some of which are just 50 microns across and 12 microns thick. For those you might need more than 2,100 pieces—and a whole lot of patience—to build a one-inch stack.

With so many sizes and shapes and types of glitter,
no wonder it has had so many uses:

toys and T-shirts,

makeup and
motorcycles,

bicycle helmets and
bowling balls,

shoes, glues,
inks, paints,

speedboats,

parade floats,

party supplies,

carnival rides,

and on, and on, and *on*.

From sparkly cupcakes to shimmery syrup, there's even glitter we can safely eat.

The ingredients in edible glitter may not sound all that appetizing. Maltodextrin, anyone? Pearlescent pigment? How about FD&C Blue No. 2? But we can consume them—and digest them.

And if the glitter is digestible . . . Well, let's just say there won't be anything special to see at the other end.

To some people glitter has become an especially big deal.

In the 1960s far-out entertainers in New York City, followed by hippie drag performers in San Francisco, began using glitter to amp up the out-of-the-ordinary nature of their shows.

By the early 1970s rock musicians were performing with glitter on their faces, hair, and bodies.

For decades glitter-decorated coconuts and shoes have been prized souvenirs during the annual Mardi Gras celebration in New Orleans.

On the day after Mardi Gras, Ash Wednesday, many Christian churchgoers are marked with ashes on their foreheads. To signal the welcoming of LGBTQ+ worshippers, some congregations now offer a mix of ashes and purple glitter.

Glitter truly is everywhere!

And it *gets* everywhere, too!

Glitter clings to your clothes, your hair, your hand.
Try to brush it off, and it clings to your other hand.
It clings to things because of static electricity.

Glitter generally has a negative electrical charge. Skin, hair, and fabric tend to be positively charged. Opposite charges attract, so when glitter comes into contact with one of those surfaces, it sticks. And it's so lightweight that it will likely stay put until a stronger force (say, a washcloth or a vacuum cleaner) comes along.

POSITIVE CHARGE

NEGATIVE CHARGE

Why, I wouldn't be surprised if there's one of those persistent little sparkles on you right now. Go ahead and check. I'll be right here, sticking around like a speck of—oh, you know.

Besides getting everywhere, glitter has other, more serious downsides.

"Microplastics" is the term for flecks of plastic that find their way into rivers, lakes, and oceans—and into the bodies of aquatic animals who mistake these bits for food.

While it took more than glitter—a lot more—to form the Great Pacific Garbage Patch, much of that massive collection of trash in the Pacific Ocean is microplastics. Every trace of plastic kept out of the water helps limit the spread of the problem.

There aren't many things that the word "microplastic" fits better than glitter. That's really nothing new: glitter has been both micro and plastic ever since Henry F. Ruschmann set up shop on Meadowbrook Farm.

What *is* new is the global conversation about whether there should be a ban on glitter because of the toll it takes on the environment.

Should the solution be NO MORE GLITTER? Maybe not. After all, if humans are drawn to things that sparkle, how well would that approach work?

What if, instead, we took our attraction to iridescent beauty, combined it with our natural problem-solving ability, and came up with safer ways to shine?

That, in fact, is what's happening.

TREES

Do these new types of glitter live up to their promise? Scientists have found that some types of biodegradable glitter still harm aquatic life. What's more, some glitter manufacturers may be dishonest about how biodegradable their glitter is.

Glittering responsibly takes more than just choosing products that look ecofriendly or claim to be biodegradable. We need to know what the science says and insist that glitter makers prove their claims.

CELLULOSE FILM

GLITTER

There are now biodegradable glitters that are made of cellulose from plants, including the fast-growing eucalyptus tree (koalas' favorite food). The idea is that these should break down naturally in soil or water before they ever make it inside an aquatic creature.

Mica has also gotten more attention recently, though it's not all favorable.

Consumers of mica-based makeup are learning to check where their cosmetics come from and to avoid unethical manufacturers or those that can't confirm that child labor was not involved.

Yes, mica is a naturally occurring alternative to plastic glitter. It's often used in cosmetics. But in India mica is mined by thousands of young children who are working to support their families rather than attending school.

It's an illegal and dangerous occupation, and kids get hurt—sometimes even killed. No amount of shimmer is worth that.

In response, some cosmetics makers have worked to ensure that the mica they use was not mined by children. Others have begun using synthetic mica that comes from laboratories.

Another alternative comes from bugs. (Yes, bugs. Again!)

As it turns out, the ancient Egyptians may have been onto something when they decorated Tutankhamun's sticks with beetle wings. We can thank another type of insect for a key ingredient in some biodegradable glitter.

In India, China, and Southeast Asia, lac scales eat tree sap and turn it into resin. They lay their eggs in the resin, which hardens and protects them. After the young have hatched, people collect the leftover resin and refine it into flakes called shellac. Shellac has been used to make a shiny coating for new kinds of glitter.

While not everyone loves glitter, even those who aren't into the stuff can be encouraged by the steps humans are taking to shimmer more thoughtfully.

So, remember how iridescence makes glitter appear different depending on our perspective?

Well, what we think about glitter also has to do with how we look at it. There are lots of possible angles. But from each point of view, one thing is constant: what makes glitter sparkle is how it catches the light.

As we come up with better ways of glittering, our cleverness and creativity make us shine, too.

Our human ingenuity is as remarkable—and persistent!—as any glitter we can imagine.

Author's Note

Glitter Everywhere? At times while I was researching and writing this book, *Glitter Everyone* seemed more like it. I had so many questions for so many people.

Those who generously helped provide answers included children of the founders of Meadowbrook Inventions, Magic Sparkles, and Glitterex; several local libraries and historical societies in New Jersey; marvelous staff members at the New Jersey State Library, the American Museum of Natural History, and the Gladys Marcus Library at the Fashion Institute of Technology; members of the Tutankhamun's Sticks and Staves Project; a curator at the Metropolitan Museum of Art; the founder of the Makeup Museum; experts in antique fishing lures; a member of New Orleans's Krewe of Muses (who happens to be a school librarian, and who teamed up with another Muse-librarian to create a glitter-covered shoe especially for me); two entomologists; an etymologist; and the head of the team that conducted the first study of the effects of biodegradable glitter on freshwater ecosystems.

I consulted dozens of articles and books, cast my eyes upon the many (many, *many*, MANY) glittery offerings at a craft store near my home in Austin, Texas, and made a fruitful trip to New Jersey and New York, where I divided my time between researching in libraries and seeing the sights in the towns where the two leading glitter companies are located. I also ate glitter-covered cupcakes and glitter-filled pancake syrup because I knew my readers would be disappointed if I didn't. (And because they were delicious.)

It was fascinating and fun, and I learned so much. But along the way I was also reminded of just how easy it can be to get a story wrong. Especially where technical details are involved, there's a danger that authors will rephrase a factual statement in a way that we *think* is correct but that actually makes it inaccurate. Writers at all levels should be super careful about that.

And in our research we should also pay attention to where each particular fact comes from, even one that we encounter in multiple places. For instance, I could find no evidence for claims—repeated by lots of writers and included in many online articles about glitter— that the ancient Egyptians ground up beetles to make a shimmery powder, or that they used this powder to create makeup. No matter how true an unsubstantiated "fact" might sound, including it in a piece of writing makes it hard for readers to trust the rest of what that writer says.

Here's something that you definitely *can* trust: my own personal statement about how I feel about glitter. Which is . . . I'm not sure. I wouldn't call myself a fan, but I don't loathe it, either. I'd prefer not to get much on me (unless it comes from the occasional cupcake), but I do understand that glitter brings joy to others. More than anything—especially after learning so much about it—I find glitter interesting, and I look forward to seeing where it goes from here.

Illustrator's Note

Illustrating this book took me back to my childhood obsession with glitter. As a kid I went through phases where I used glitter glue in all my art projects and wrote my notes for school exclusively in glittery ink. I carried a schoolbag with a glittery gel decoration—until the teachers discovered that it stained everything (and everyone) with glitter and banned it. Luckily I still had my glittery pencil case.

Despite my fond memories of glitter, I was saddened to learn about how it impacts the lives of children forced into labor in India. Reading about new types of safe and ethical glitter gives me hope. And while I may no longer write my to-do lists in glitter ink, I find myself adding dots, sparkles, and flecks to all my digital illustrations, trying to recreate the magic of craft glitter.

For Further Reading

The Big Book of Bling: Ritzy Rocks, Extravagant Animals, Sparkling Science, and More! by Rose Davidson (National Geographic, 2019)

Bonkers About Beetles by Owen Davey (Flying Eye Books, 2018)

My Book of Rocks and Minerals by Devin Dennie (DK, 2017)

Plastic, Ahoy! Investigating the Great Pacific Garbage Patch by Patricia Newman, photographs by Annie Crawley (Millbrook, 2014)

Plastic: Past, Present, and Future by Eun-ju Kim, illustrated by Ji-won Lee (Scribble, 2019)

A Ray of Light: A Book of Science and Wonder by Walter Wick (Scholastic, 2019)

The Secrets of Tutankhamun: Egypt's Boy King and His Incredible Tomb by Patricia Cleveland-Peck, illustrated by Isabel Greenberg (Bloomsbury, 2018)

The Way Things Work Now: From Levers to Lasers, Windmills to Wi-Fi, a Visual Guide to the World of Machines by David Macaulay (Houghton Mifflin Harcourt, 2016)

Selected Bibliography

Bernardsville News. "Bertha E. Ruschmann." March 27, 2009. https://www.newjerseyhills.com/bernardsville_news/obituaries/bertha-e-ruschmann/article_18cf71b3-22b9-550d-8b2c-3062e53f471b.html.

Bernardsville News. "Maplewood Man Buys Local Estate: H. F. Ruschmann Purchases Meadow Brook Farm in Mine Brook Road from Paul F. Freytag." November 18, 1943.

Bramley, Ellie Violet. "Losing Its Sparkle: The Dark Side of Glitter." *Guardian*, January 21, 2018. https://www.theguardian.com/fashion/2018/jan/21/losing-its-sparkle-the-dark-side-of-glitter.

Campbell, Colin. "On Ash Wednesday, a Symbol Gets an Update." *Baltimore Sun*, March 2, 2017.

Esposito, Frank. "Glitterex Adds Space, Sparkle." *Plastics News*, May 3, 1999.

Fiedler, Lore. "The Glitter Factory Brightens the Season." *Courier-News*, December 17, 1979.

Green, Dannielle Senga, Megan Jefferson, Bas Boots, and Leon Stone. Abstract for "All That Glitters Is Litter? Ecological Impacts of Conventional versus Biodegradable Glitter in a Freshwater Habitat." *Journal of Hazardous Materials* 402 (2021). doi:10.1016/j.jhazmat.2020.124070.

Holmes, Soline. "Two Glittering Librarians & Their Storybook Shoes!" *ALSC Matters!*, August 2019.

McLeod, Kembrew. *The Downtown Pop Underground: New York City and the Literary Punks, Renegade Artists, DIY Filmmakers, Mad Playwrights, and Rock 'n' Roll Glitter Queens Who Revolutionized Culture*. New York: Abrams, 2018.

Meadows, Melissa G., et al. "Iridescence: Views from Many Angles." *Interface Focus* 6 (2009): S107–S113. doi:10.1098/rsif.2009.0013.focus.

The URLs listed here were accurate at publication, but websites often change. If a URL doesn't work, you can use the internet to find more information.

Meert, Katrien, Mario Pandelaere, and Vanessa M. Patrick. "Taking a Shine to It: How the Preference for Glossy Stems from an Innate Need for Water." *Journal of Consumer Psychology* 24 (2013). doi:10.1016/j.jcps.2013.12.005.

New Jersey State Industrial Directory, 1960–1961 Edition. New York: New Jersey State Industrial Directory, 1960.

Philo, Simon. *Glam Rock: Music in Sound and Vision*. Lanham, MD: Rowman & Littlefield, 2018.

Rivers, Victoria Z. *The Shining Cloth: Dress and Adornment That Glitter*. New York: Thames & Hudson, 1999.

Ruschmann, Henry F. *Operating Upon Sheets of Foil*. US Patent 3,156,283, filed February 14, 1961, and issued November 10, 1964.

Seago, Ainsley E., Parrish Brady, Jean-Pol Vigneron, and Tom D. Schultz. "Gold Bugs and Beyond: A Review of Iridescence and Structural Colour Mechanisms in Beetles (Coleoptera)." *Interface Focus* 6 (2009): S165–S184. doi:10.1098/rsif.2008.0354.focus.

Shaw, Mary Louise. "Ruschmann Wants to Expand, and an Old Fuss Is Recalled." *Bernardsville News*, March 16, 1978.

Stuart, Sandy. "Most of The World's Glitter Comes from This Quiet, Conservative Town." *Bernardsville News*, December 16, 1982.

Veldmeijer, André J., and Salima Ikram. "Tutankhamun's Sticks and Staves: The Importance of Deceptively Simple Objects." *Scribe* 5 (2020): 8–13.

Wayland, Russell G. "Mica in War." *American Institute of Mining and Metallurgical Engineers Technical Publication* No. 1749, February 1944.

Weaver, Caity. "What Is Glitter?" *New York Times*, December 21, 2018.

Weinberg, Caroline. "Everything You Need to Know About Eating Glitter." *Eater*, December 17, 2018. https://www.eater.com/2018/2/14/17008460/edible-glitter-non-toxic-glitter-explained.

Please visit **https://chrisbarton.info/books/glitter** for a complete bibliography.